Contents

INTRODUCTION	
HISTORY OF BAT BOXES	
TYPES AND CONSTRUCTION OF	
Summer boxes	4
Size	5
Material	5
Thickness of walls	6
Entry slit	6
Construction	8
Top, side or front opening	8
Exterior finish	8
Concrete boxes	8
Winter (hibernation) boxes	9
FIXING METHODS	10
SITING	11
Height above ground	12
Aspect	13
Distribution	14
Area and tree choice	14
Altitude	14
Urban areas	15
INSPECTION OF BOXES	16
Timing	16
Signs of use	17
Checking for bats	17
Check-list of equipment needed for inspection	18
IDENTIFICATION OF BATS	19
PROBLEMS - of Decay and Competition	19
SURVEY AND RESEARCH	20
EXPERIMENTAL DESIGNS	20
LICENSING	20
Wildlife and Countryside Act 1981	20
When to apply for a licence	20
BAT BOX PROJECT - Institute of Terrestrial Ecology, BBC TV *Nationwide*, Forestry Commission and WWF	22
BIBLIOGRAPHY	24
USEFUL ADDRESSES	24
ACKNOWLEDGEMENTS	Inside back cover

BAT BOXES

Bat boxes are purpose-built artificial holes or crevices providing roost sites for bats. They are used primarily to aid the conservation of bats where natural roost sites are few or absent. **Correct siting is crucial to their success in being adopted by bats, but also shape and design are important.**

Bats will roost in boxes for much of the year, sometimes roosting solitarily but nursery clusters of several species have occurred, with up to 65 bats in one box.

The purpose of this booklet is to provide a practical guide to all aspects of the theory, construction, siting and inspection of bat boxes.

INTRODUCTION

In Britain bats are mostly secretive, forest-dwelling animals, which have adapted to, or have been affected by, the changing pattern of habitats. They all feed on insects, which are now much reduced in numbers as a result of changing agricultural practice and land use.

Tree loss, especially of old hollow trees, has greatly reduced the availability of roost sites and has increased competition amongst hole-dwelling animals. Direct conflict occurs between some species with, for example, starlings driving out and killing bats from old woodpecker holes.

Bats move from site to site seasonally and are inquisitive animals, constantly investigating potential roosts. It is not known why a particular roost is chosen, but it needs to have an adequate temperature regime, to be close to suitable feeding areas and to be secluded and safe from predators. A large proportion of bats roost individually or in small groups and need only cracks and crevices, but nursery clusters require larger spaces.

Bats use all kinds of sites, including old woodpecker holes, caves, mines and buildings. They are known to hide among the tangle of branches in yew and other trees, amongst ivy and behind loose bark. They have been found in badger setts and some probably enter the burrows of other animals such as foxes and rabbits, especially in rocky areas. They occur in rock crevices in cliffs and quarries, in dry stone walls and probably roost in mountain scree slopes as they do in similar rock piles in caves. Disused railway, canal and other tunnels are often important roosts, together with ice-houses and underground passages around fortifications and large country houses.

Most species of British bats have adapted to roosting in buildings for at least part of the year, where they have often been killed by people through intolerance, or incidentally by the chemicals used in 'woodworm' treatment. Indeed, remedial timber treatment has been a major cause of the observed declines in some species.

To some extent, bat boxes can redress the loss of roost sites, but **they must be constructed and sited carefully** if they are to stand a reasonable chance of being used. At least 11 of the 15 British species of bat are known to have roosted in boxes in Britain or Europe. Only the two horseshoe bats are unlikely to be found in either boxes or hollow trees.

HISTORY OF BAT BOXES

A description of boxes provided for bats was published in France in 1918. Within 20 years, the principle of providing artificial roosts was well established, especially in central and eastern Europe. Bats, together with insectivorous birds, were recognised as being predators on insect pests in conifer plantations and because these forests were almost devoid of natural roosts, boxes were provided. Tens of thousands of boxes were installed and a huge array of different designs were tried, many of which were elaborate and costly to manufacture. Experimentation in shape, size and material still continues, but the relative success of such experiments is poorly documented. Generally, insufficient attention has been given to the careful siting of boxes, and may have accounted for the poor success of some projects. However, a number of publications in the last 30 years have detailed the most useful designs and their success.

In Britain, in May 1968, the first boxes (26) were positioned in Dorset, and within five months the first bat was found. It was known bats had visited several boxes before that date because droppings had been found in them.

As a result of this pilot project, a larger scheme was devised by the Institute of Terrestrial Ecology in conjunction with the BBC TV, the Forestry Commission and the World Wildlife Fund. Over 3,000 boxes were installed in six forests from northern Scotland to southern England. Two experiments were terminated in 1982, another in 1986, but three have been extended considerably and each now covers tens of square kilometres.

The advice contained in this leaflet is based on the results of these projects as well as of other successful projects in several European countries.

TYPES AND CONSTRUCTION OF BAT BOXES

Because of the variety of sites in which bats are found, a wide range of box shapes have been built. There are likely to be plenty of natural holes and crevices which will accommodate individuals or small groups, but larger clusters of bats probably lack suitable numbers of alternative roosts. Therefore, it could be a waste of effort catering for individual bats, instead, resources ought to be devoted to providing roosts especially for breeding clusters. The boxes discussed here will be used by individuals as well as by clusters.

Summer boxes

These are made with relatively thin walls (about 20-30mm thick) and are used by bats throughout the year except when winter temperatures fall below about minus 4°C. In lowland areas, boxes are used mostly from April to November. At higher altitudes (300m+) they may be used only from late May to September.

Size - internal dimensions

The aim is to construct boxes which allow clusters of adequate size to develop. **This is essential because bats in nurseries must be able to cluster in order to conserve heat** (see also **Siting boxes** page 11). The minimum effective internal volume is 100 x 100 x 100mm. Larger boxes may be made, but 100mm should always be maintained as the front-to-back measurement, because many bat species prefer to cluster in confined spaces. Boxes with only 20-30mm front-to-back are little used except by males, which prefer cooler conditions and sometimes females are attracted in autumn for mating. (These flat boxes are used more commonly in warmer countries, for example near the Mediterranean where clustering of bats is less important). Both height and width may usefully be increased. The width should not exceed 150mm but height may be increased to 300mm or more. These volumes will allow roosting by clusters numbering from 40 to 100 bats of a medium-sized species like the brown long-eared bat *Plecotus auritus*. The higher, larger-size boxes are most appropriate for the large noctules *Nyctalus noctula*.

The most successful boxes for general use have internal measurements of 100mm front to back, are 150mm wide and from 120-180mm high with a well-fitted sloping roof.

Materials

Most boxes have been made with softwood - spruce, fir and pine - which may decay or split and are easily damaged by woodpeckers and squirrels. For general use, this is the cheapest and most reliable material. Boxes made of these timbers generally last about ten years. Weathered rough-surfaced roof-felt may be used to cover tops.

No wood preservatives should be used as many are harmful to bats.

Boxes made with elm *Ulmus spp.* have been successful but generally this tough, long-lasting timber has been little used because it warps and therefore adequate seals against draughts and rain are difficult to maintain.

It is most important to ensure the box is well made and free of gaps which could let in draughts or rain.

The cedar *Cedrus libani* does not rot, but because this wood has had limited use, we do not know whether it is particularly attractive to bats. The strong odour and soft texture may be avoided. The redwoods, eg *Sequoiadendron giganteum* produce excellent rot free, light weight, odourless timber, which has proved suitable, but this wood is expensive and difficult to obtain.

Thickness of walls

There is a need to compromise between thin walls which warm up quickly and thicker ones which provide some insulation and will retain the heat of clustered bats. The timber should be 25mm or slightly thicker. **The wood needs to be roughsawn or roughened** on all surfaces so that bats are able to land and investigate by crawling all over the box. If the wood is relatively smooth, horizontal saw cuts should be made about one millimetre deep on the inside and around the entrance. Bats have sharp claws on their toes which can grip even very tiny projections.

Entry slit

The hole should be at the bottom of the box and either in the front or in the base, with a rough surrounding landing area.

Slit size should be a minimum of 15 x 40mm long, but generally it is easiest to construct a slit running the width of the box. With these long slits the gap needs to be between 15 to 18mm wide. Larger slits will let in birds (especially tits and tree-creepers) which often nest in bat boxes.

Plank: 1,135mm x 150mm x 25mm (10mm allowed for saw cuts)

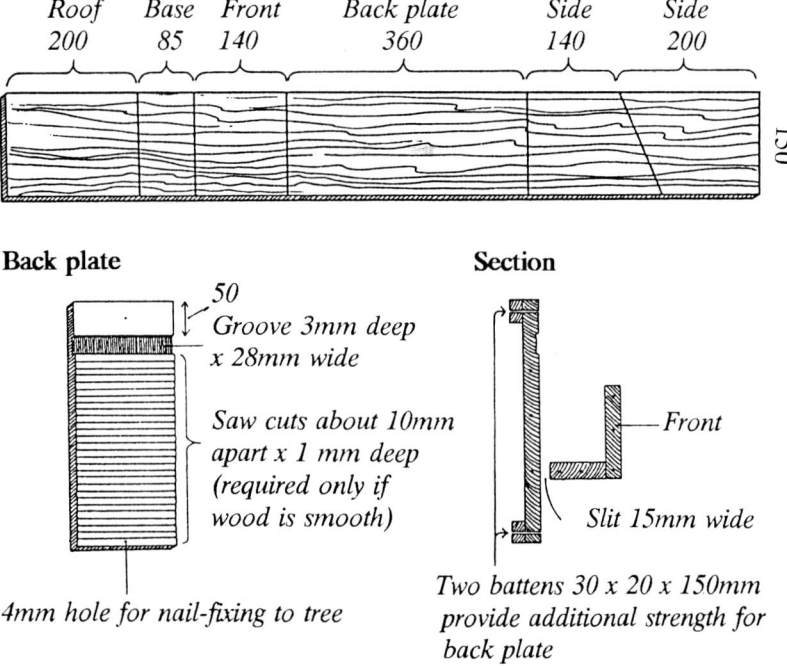

All dimensions in millimetres

Roof	Base	Front	Back plate	Side	Side
200	85	140	360	140	200

150

Back plate

50
Groove 3mm deep x 28mm wide

Saw cuts about 10mm apart x 1 mm deep (required only if wood is smooth)

4mm hole for nail-fixing to tree

Section

Front

Slit 15mm wide

Two battens 30 x 20 x 150mm provide additional strength for back plate

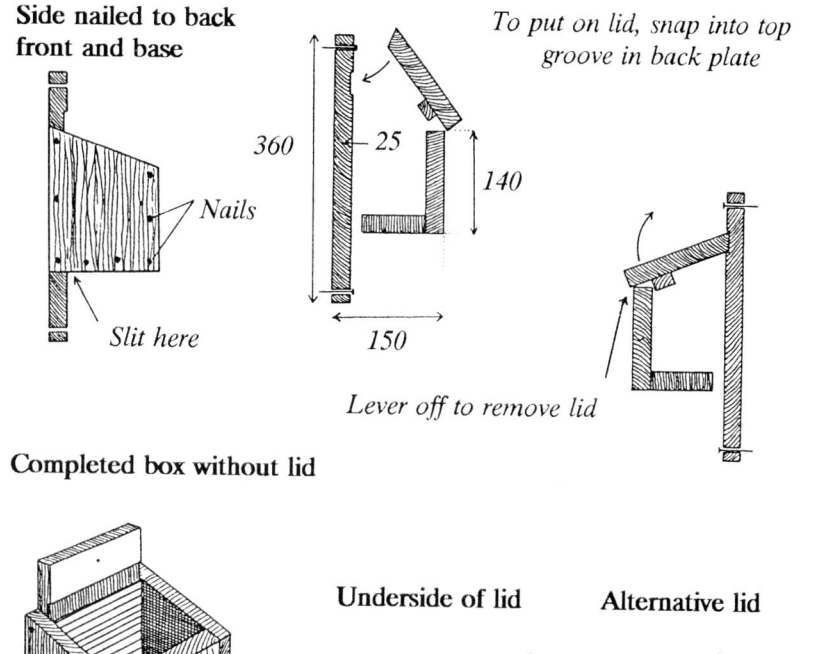

Figure 1 Bat Box Construction
Softwood should be rough all over. Saw cuts on the back plate are only necessary if the wood is smooth.

The groove cut in the top of the back plate is to take the lid, which snaps into it. Alternatively, make a hinge for the lid. A strip of tyre inner tube may be tacked to lid and backplate and a wire hook can be fitted to the front. A hook will help prevent animals or wind lifting the lid, especially if the wood shrinks or warps. Rubber bands made from inner tubes may be used to hold on lids.

Alternative construction suggestions
a. Fix top firmly and provide a loose fitting bottom hinged at the front. This is held in place by a length of galvanised wire (about 3mm diameter) placed in an oversized drill hole at one side. When the wire is withdrawn the bottom drops by gravity. Take care from March to July because birds could be nesting.

b. A vertical partition of 10mm thick rough timber can be inserted side to side in the box leaving 40mm space above the base. It is best to provide this ONLY in large boxes.

A well fitting lid greatly improves the chances of the boxes being used by bats.

Construction

The two important considerations are internal dimensions and thickness of wood.

Figure 1 shows the construction details for the most successful and well tried design. One box requires a plank of timber 1,135 x 150 x 25mm and a batten 25 x 15 x 120mm to hold the lid on. The box may be glued using a waterproof resin glue, but fixing by nails is quicker and much simpler. (Blunting the nail points before using helps prevent the wood splitting).

The lid needs the batten attaching to the underside front so that when putting the lid on the box the front is placed down first, allowing the rear to be snapped into the groove in the back plate. When removing the lid the front should be lifted first.

An alternative to using the batten to hold on the lid - which requires great care to position correctly - is to fit hooks and eyes or similar catches. Strips of car inner tube nailed to the top and back plate can be used to form a weatherproof hinge, but this makes safe removal of bats more difficult.

Top, side or front opening?

Front or side opening boxes have the advantage of needing less skill to fit the lid accurately. However, they have a serious drawback. When opening on a warm day with a cluster of bats hanging on the door, most bats fly away immediately and others may be injured as the door may be quickly closed.

Exterior finish

Paints or preservatives must not be used as these may be toxic or deter bats from adopting the box because of the odours or a smooth surface. Roof felt, especially the thicker type with rough, stone-chip covered surface, can be attached to the lid to shed water but should not cover the box entirely. There may be advantages in the boxes being dark colours so as to absorb heat quicker by day. Dark vegetable dyes may be used but no conclusive benefit has been demonstrated. **A darkened exterior makes new boxes less conspicuous** and hence may reduce vandalism.

Concrete boxes

Boxes constructed of a cement and sawdust mixture are gaining popularity in some Europe countries but few have been tried in Britain. Bats will adopt them and they have the advantage of being rot-free and more or less proof against attack from woodpeckers and squirrels, but they are difficult and expensive to make, especially in small numbers. The British Trust for Ornithology's Field Guide No. 3 (Nest Boxes), gives details of how to make concrete/sawdust boxes for birds, and Batchat No 9 (obtainable from English Nature) gives details of these boxes for bats.

Ready-made concrete bat boxes can be purchased from Schwegler-Vogelschutzgeräte GmbH, Heinkelstraße 35, 7060 Schorndorf, Germany.

Winter (hibernation) boxes

Boxes designed for hibernation are positioned in forests and some have been used by a small number of bats. Criteria for designs are based on known natural holes in trees where bats hibernate (**Figure 2**). The only substantial difference from summer boxes is the need to provide sufficient wall thickness to insulate bats from extremes of cold. Clustered bats in hibernation utilise body fat to generate some heat when temperatures fall below freezing, but with insufficient insulation they would probably awaken and move off to select a better roost.

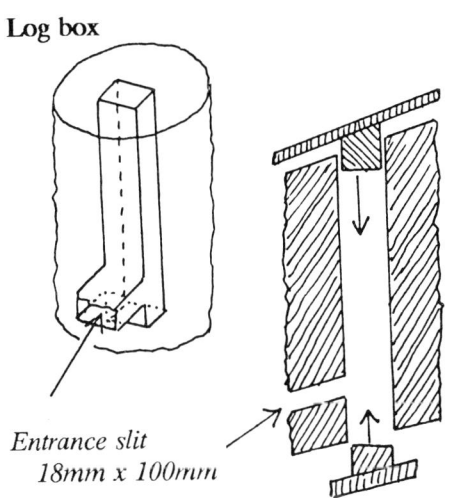

Log box

Entrance slit
18mm x 100mm

Figure 2 Hibernation Box Construction

Examples of hibernation box designs currently being tried. All have a central hole about 100mm square and 300mm high internally (with the top permanently fitted) and not less than 100mm thickness of material surrounding the cavity. The base is removable to allow inspection without greatly disturbing the bats.

Sandwich box

Wood framework with vermiculite or weathered expanded polystyrene or other inert insulation material

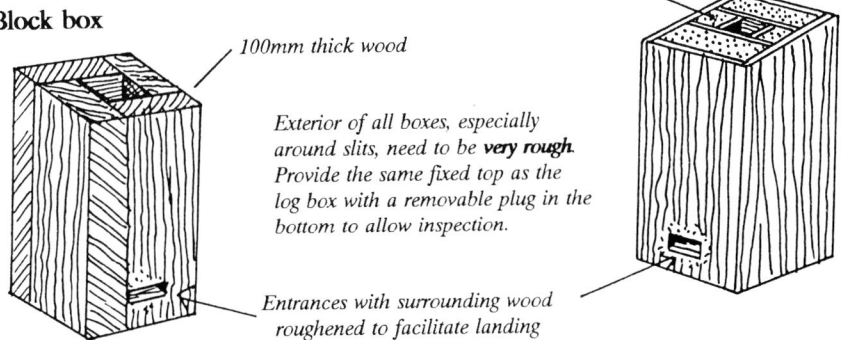

Block box

100mm thick wood

*Exterior of all boxes, especially around slits, need to be **very rough**. Provide the same fixed top as the log box with a removable plug in the bottom to allow inspection.*

Entrances with surrounding wood roughened to facilitate landing

In winter, hollow branches cut off trees during tidying-up operations in the woods and parks have been found to contain bats. The bats are usually at the apex of the hole and generally have 80-100mm of timber on the thinnest side. Winter boxes have been made by hollowing out suitably sized logs, or with 100mm thick planking. Such boxes are very heavy, so lighter boxes, made by sandwiching vermiculite or polystyrene (weathered to remove odours) between 20mm thick wood, are also being tested. Full details for building hibernation boxes are not given here because the idea is relatively new and untried and more experimentation is required before large scale installation can be recommended. Felled hollow branches or tree trunks, especially those known to have contained bats may be repositioned on other trees. Tops should be fixed but bases removable to allow inspection without disturbing or waking bats.

FIXING METHODS

The selected method will depend on a variety of criteria. Boxes are intended for attachment to trees, and the owner of the trees must be consulted about the fixing method. The size of project, species of tree and ultimate use of the tree will influence the decision.

The aim is to attach the boxes safely and firmly. In several European countries some, especially concrete boxes, have been hung by wire from branches. These boxes sway in the wind and are occupied less than those rigidly fixed. Nailing is the simplest and cheapest method, and iron nails may be used on all trees which are not destined for the commercial market. The Forestry Commission has recommended copper nails on plantation conifers, but new trials suggest aluminium alloy nails may be better. These soft metal nails are said not to damage saws or chipping machinery. Copper nails have not been used on commercial hardwoods because of the suggestion they may poison trees. However, no proof has been found. A trial to investigate this, involving copper nails being driven into the trunks of oak and ash, shows no evidence of debilitation of any tree after 14 years. A land-owner may be willing to designate a few hardwood trees in plantations as 'amenity', effectively writing them off and thereby allowing the use of iron nails.

Usually it is impossible to pull out nails so it is best to use more or less headless ones (eg barrel-headed), which allow the growing tree to push off the box. A large-headed nail often causes the back plate of the box to break, necessitating a repair. Conifers may put on over ten millimetres radius each year and some boxes will need re-nailing at least every second year.

Instead of using nails, boxes may be fixed using hardwood dowelling, which requires drilling slightly undersized holes in the tree and box. The dowel may be quite long to enable the box to be pushed along the projecting end for several years, as the tree thickens.

Figure 3 Method of fixing box to accommodate growth. Especially useful for heavy hibernation boxes.

The box is mounted with horizontal 'wings' wider than the tree's diameter - allowing for, say, 10 years growth. On the other side of the tree a similar length wing is drilled at either end through which the rods are placed. Springs on the rod followed by washers and the wing-nuts allow growth to be accommodated without the constant need to slacken the nuts. This method is especially useful for the heavy hibernation boxes which also can be sited resting on a stump of a sawn-off side branch.

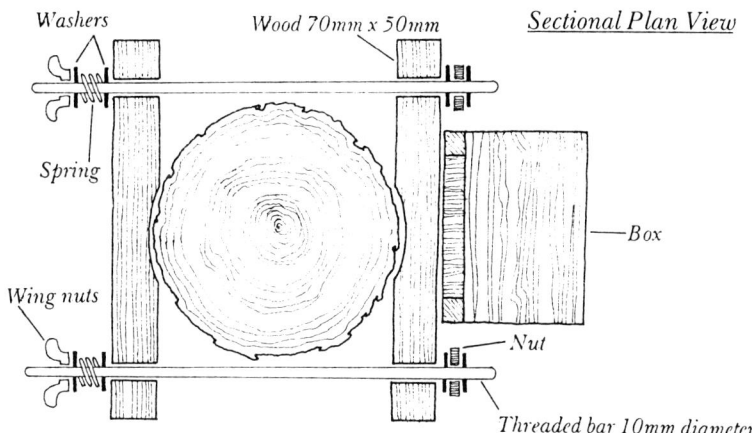

Tied bands of cord or wire attached to the top and bottom of the boxes allow frequent readjustment during tree growth, but they have the disadvantage of generally providing a less firm fixing. A more elaborate and expensive fixing may be made by using long threaded lengths of stainless steel or brass rod with wing-nuts and springs (**Figure 3**).

SITING

Careful siting of boxes is crucial to their success.

Generally, there should be no crowding branches or other obstructions beside, in front, or below boxes for at least three metres in each direction, and no leafy branches should be within one metre above the box. It is best to site boxes in places where they can be easily refound and inspected, such as close to rides.

Height above ground

A greater number of species will use high boxes rather than those near the ground. Boxes 1.5m above the ground will be used by long-eared bats and a few other species, but noctules prefer boxes at least five metres high.

The aim should be to position boxes as high as is convenient. This will depend upon size and height of trees, height of ladder, and likelihood of vandalism, remembering that people on horseback can readily reach 4-5m above the ground.

Choice of ladder is most important, especially for larger schemes. Normally at least two people should always be present for installation and inspection of boxes when using ladders. Safety helmets should be worn and this is a requirement for approved projects on Forestry Commission land. There have been several accidents and many near misses resulting from boxes or hammers accidentally dropping five metres or more.

The best ladders are made of lightweight, but rigid, alloy single section or with two sections and splayed at the bottom to provide stability. The top rung needs material wrapping around to prevent slipping on narrow tree trunks. Use, for example, an old motor cycle inner tube.

The assistant should always firmly hold and stand on the bottom of the ladder and the person attaching boxes should be clipped (for example with a karabiner) or tied to the ladder with a strong belt or strap leaving both hands free for work.

Figure 4. Plan of recommended layout of boxes per tree.

Aspect

Where possible, boxes should be installed to provide a variety of aspects. If fewer than ten boxes are to be fixed, site them facing from south-east to south-west so sun falls on most of them for part of the day. In larger projects it is best to provide three boxes per tree arranged at the same height but facing north, south-east and south-west. This ensures a range of temperature regimes is available. It is essential for most boxes with a southerly aspect to receive direct sun for part of the day. This may entail removing shading branches above boxes.

Bats often reduce their energy expenditure by selecting boxes warmed by the sun. This is especially important for pregnant females and later for the weanlings. During very hot weather, boxes facing north may be used in preference to those in direct sun. Having several boxes on one tree allows bats to move during the day without the risk of predation.

Distribution

In larger projects, five or six trees should be selected within about 50m radius with three boxes per tree (**Figure 4**). The pattern should be repeated at approximately one kilometre intervals. However, for conservation management purposes the chosen sites should depend more upon their appropriateness for bats than rigid adherence to a grid.

Area and tree choice

The best areas to site boxes are those where bats regularly feed but which are devoid of other roosts. They need to be sheltered from strong winds and exposed to the sun. Generally, glades are good areas especially close to marshland and rivers or ponds. Valley bottoms are better than the sides or hilltops, and boxes beside wide rides are more often occupied than those along narrow paths.

Site and tree selection is best done on a sunny day when it should be obvious which are the warmest and most sheltered areas. Boxes are most assured of early occupancy by bats when placed in the centre of large forests, far away from hollow trees or buildings, which often provide alternative roost sites. But boxes may be adopted in almost any situation.

Despite the superficial uniformity of plantations, there are usually individual trees which stand out from their neighbours. Such trees may act as focal points for all kinds of wildlife, including the insects which bats eat, hence, boxes placed in these positions are possibly more likely to be found. Sometimes a few crowding branches will need to be cut away.

In the management of the forest crop, larger trees are more likely to remain until final clear felling, while other adjacent trees may be felled during thinning. About a year before an area is clear-felled adjacent areas should have boxes installed to allow time for 'weathering in' and for the bats to find them.

Altitude

High-altitude locations in Britain (above 300m) are usually considered unsuitable for bats. However, boxes placed in a relatively poor site at that elevation upon a hillside on the Scottish/English border and a hill top in northern Scotland, were used by a few bats of at least five species. Bats are known to hibernate in caves and mines up to 650m in northern England and Scotland.

Urban Areas

A few boxes are known to have been used when placed in gardens and on houses but there is no accurate picture of their relative success. (See also *Inspection of Boxes* below). Also, bats are known to occupy holes in telegraph poles beside roads. Boxes so placed may be used but the owners permission must be gained before starting such a project.

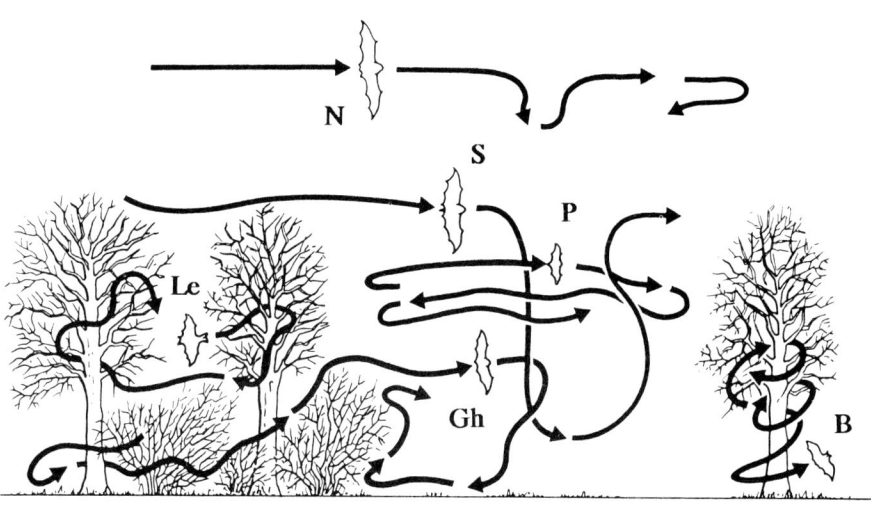

Key - bat species

N	-	noctule	P - pipistrelle		B	- Bechstein's
S	-	serotine	Le - brown long-eared		Gh	- greater horseshoe

Figure 5

Each bat species feeds in a different way, with some like long-eared and Bechstein's bats hunting within woodland often amongst foliage, while Natterer's feed along rides or close to hedgerows, and others such as pipistrelle and noctule being predominantly found in open areas.

However, bats change their hunting strategies to suit the availability and distribution of their insect food. While feeding may be mostly well above ground early in the evening, later, when its gets cooler bats frequently fly to ground to catch insects.

(After an original drawing by R E Stebbings in **Bats***, Mammal Society Series, Anthony Nelson, Oswestry)*

INSPECTION OF BOXES (see also Licensing)

Because acceptance of boxes by bats is much less predictable than for birds, it is essential to inspect boxes frequently so that, in time, those unused may be repositioned. Groups of boxes which have not been used for two years should be repositioned. If some boxes appear unused, in an area where other boxes have been regularly occupied, then repositioning is not recommended. Bats often visit boxes without leaving any trace.

Timing

Boxes may be sited at any time but inspections should preferably be made at about six weekly intervals, from April to November, making a total of four visits per year.

Boxes must not be inspected from mid June - mid August when bats are giving birth or are lactating. Disturbance at that time can cause abortions or abandonment of young.

Bats may use boxes intermittently and the chance of finding bats in occupation will, at best, be about 1 in 10.

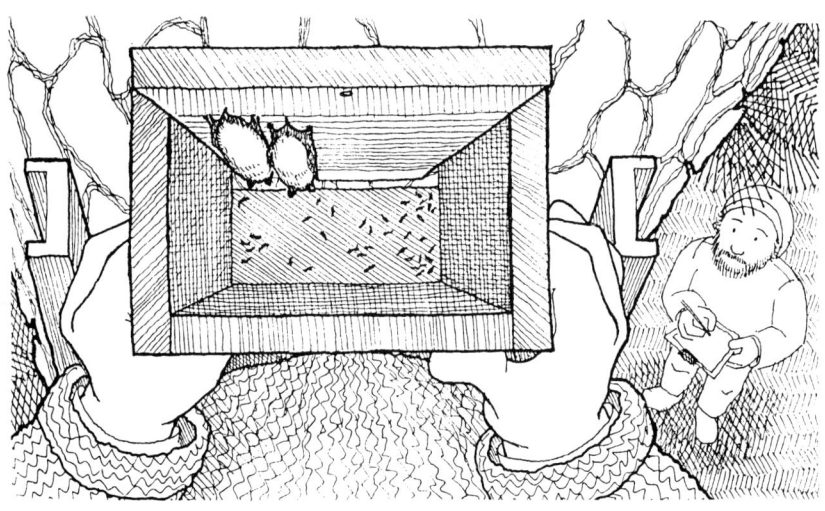

Signs of use

Bats sometimes leave droppings, which, with care, can be distinguished from bird and other droppings. Tits, treecreepers and wrens regularly use bat boxes for roosting, all are insectivorous and their droppings can resemble those of bats in shape and texture. When fresh, bird droppings usually have some white uric acid excretion at one end of the dropping, while bat droppings never have any white element. Often, bird droppings are produced in circles about 50mm diameter in the bottom of the box, with usually two circles per box, whereas bat droppings tend to be scattered and not in a regular pattern. When dry, bird droppings tend to be hard, whereas bat droppings easily crumble to reveal their fine chewed remains of insects.

Bat droppings may be black to brown and are variable in size, shape and texture. Pipistrelle droppings are the smallest, being about 1.5mm in diameter and 7-9mm long, whereas noctule droppings may be up to 4 x 10mm. There is a very wide variation in size and appearance even within one species, so identification is difficult. With practice, and by keeping samples from known species, a good indication of their identity may be obtained (see Stebbings, 1986a).

Checking for bats

When inspecting boxes they must be opened carefully because bats may be hanging on the lid or door. In order to check whether bats are present, use a torch to look through the entrance slit. During hot weather the bats will be highly active and often, will fly out of the bottom unless a hand or cloth is placed over the slit. In most cases, species identity and approximate numbers are all that is required. For non-experts, identification of bats usually requires having one in the hand so measurements may be taken and an identification key used. Checking is most convenient during the day, but can also be done at dusk using a hand held net beneath the box entrance. Bats may bite, especially inexperienced handlers, and although most species only give a little nip, a bite from the large noctule can be painful. Thin leather gloves are recommended. After identification, active bats must be released to fly off.

Bats must always be taken out of boxes before replacing the lid, but if the animals are torpid, they should be placed carefully at the entrance and allowed to crawl up into the box.

This prevents the possibility of legs or wings becoming trapped, which has caused the accidental death of some bats.

Check-list of equipment needed for bat box inspection:

Ladder
Torch - to see inside through entrance before opening.
Screwdriver to lever off tight fitting box lids.
Small cotton bags about 150 x 200mm with tie strings in which to put bats prior to identification (ensure seams are on the outside to prevent bats being entangled in threads).
Thin leather gloves eg. pilots gloves.
Ruler with which to take measurements (millimetre scale).
Bat identification guide.
Record sheets or notebook.
Box location map.
Tools and materials for repairs eg. hammer, nails, wood spares/glue.
Hard hat.
Small rigid containers for dropping samples.
Camera to photograph bats facial characters if identity is uncertain.

IDENTIFICATION OF BATS

Critical identification will be achieved using the key in *Which Bat Is It?* (Stebbings, 1986a). An indication of species identity often may be obtained by comparing bats facial characters with photographs such as those in Schober and Grimburger, (1989).

PROBLEMS - of decay and competition

Box decay: **No preservations should be used on the boxes because the chemicals may harm bats**, but average life of softwood boxes is about ten years. Some wood is prone to splitting, but often splits can be repaired easily with glue, wood slats or metal strapping.

As with birds' nest boxes, grey squirrels and great-spotted woodpeckers are the greatest nuisance and have destroyed large numbers of boxes, usually by enlarging the entrance at the base. One solution is to fix sheet metal to the base of each box (for example flattened food cans). A 20mm strip of metal fixed adjacent to the entry slit will sometimes be sufficient but boxes can be attacked from any angle. Sheet metal on several sides will make the box less desirable because bats will not be able to land and crawl on the smooth surfaces.

An owl, in Wareham Forest, is thought to have eaten over 100 ringed brown long-eared bats when it learnt to remove lids from boxes. This problem was solved by providing firm fixings for the lids.

Wasps can be a nuisance and a hazard, especially in northern England and Scotland. In a Scottish forest (Ardross) in 1978, 37 out of 480 boxes contained wasps' nests. Nests can be cleaned out in the winter when the wasps have died. Queen wasps and hornets hibernate in the boxes, but they usually leave before the bats return. However, wasps are highly beneficial animals and should not be killed.

Slugs, 'house' spiders, wood ants and earwigs can all discourage bats from using a box. Any box found to be persistently harbouring large numbers of such invertebrates should be repositioned.

Birds nesting in bat boxes are not a substantial problem; indeed, it can be counted as a bonus. Treecreepers are most frequent. They are very sensitive to disturbance, so try to avoid inspecting boxes containing nests. Long-eared bats have been found on several occasions roosting with fledgling treecreepers. Blue, coal and great tits have also nested in bat boxes and usually fledge successfully. Occasionally almost fledged young have been found dead through spreading the nest material until the entrance is blocked. A few wrens have nested in bat boxes but generally boxes are too exposed and too high above the ground for this species.

SURVEY AND RESEARCH

Bat boxes can aid the accumulation of information on local and national distribution of species. They can be used in the study of the population dynamics of bats in varying habitats, but such projects are expensive to set up and need to run for at least six years, but preferably ten. Bat research projects using boxes are not suitable for undergraduate or other short-term studies.

There is a need to test experimentally new designs and materials. Such projects need to be designed carefully if the results are to be meaningful. **Projects have been set up, supposedly to *test new designs* but results are likely to be meaningless unless a rigorously devised experiment is formulated.** Whether a large or small project, care should be taken to record the size and type of box, the date of installation, the exact position of each box and subsequently their contents. Negative records are just as important as successes to enable better advice to be given in future. We are keen to receive results from all bat boxes and can advise on the testing of new designs and materials. Write to *The* Robert Stebbings Consultancy Limited, 74 Alexandra Road, Peterborough PE1 3DG.

EXPERIMENTAL DESIGNS

A variety of designs are being made and sited but usually there is no measure of success. Alternative patterns should be tested alongside proven types where there is a known marked population of box-adapted bats. Any person wishing to know how 'their' boxes compare with the standard design may submit a batch of 12. These will be placed in an existing experimental area in Thetford Forest where there is a detailed knowledge of the bat population. Please contact R E Stebbings.

LICENSING

Wildlife and Countryside Act 1981

All bats and their roosts received protection under this Act and it is an offence deliberately to disturb, handle or kill bats. Inspecting bat boxes with the hope or expectation of finding bats can, therefore, be illegal without an appropriate licence.

When to apply for a licence

If a few boxes are being installed on private land and the owner is the person likely to undertake inspections, it is probably most reasonable to delay obtaining a licence until the first bats are found. As several thousand people are known to have small numbers of bat boxes in their gardens and English

Nature (formerly Nature Conservancy Council) would be inundated if all applied for licences.

Anyone undertaking larger projects, which includes putting boxes in public places or involving several people, should obtain training in bat handling and identification before applying for a licence. This should be done before the first inspection. Application forms may be obtained from the Licensing Section, English Nature, Northminster House, Peterborough, PE1 1UA.

Marking bats is also subject to licensing. When planning a project involving marking please contact Dr R E Stebbings, Ringing Secretary, The Mammal Society, c/o *The* Robert Stebbings Consultancy Limited, 74 Alexandra Road, Peterborough, PE1 3DG.

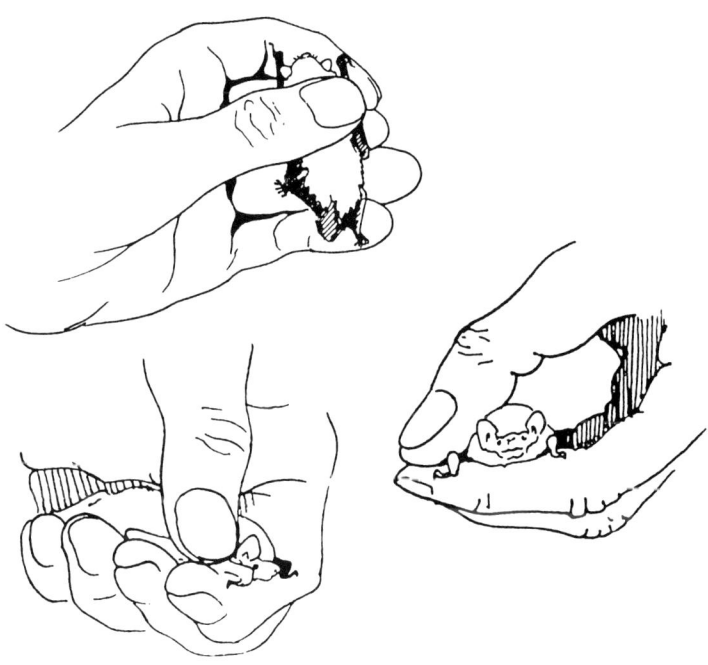

Figure 6
Bats need to be held carefully if they are not to be damaged. These illustrations show how to hold live bats for examination. However, disturbing and handling bats requires training and licensing (see this page).

(Drawings by Tom P McOwat from **Which bat is it?***)*

BAT BOX PROJECT
Institute of Terrestrial Ecology (NERC), BBC TV-*Nationwide*, Forestry Commission and World Wildlife Fund (WWF)

In 1975, the late Ronald Webster (BBC/TV producer) agreed to present an item on the *Nationwide* programme, in which people were asked to sponsor bat boxes. Robert Dougall generously helped Bob Stebbings launch the project. Only one or two hundred sponsors were expected, but over 3,000 boxes were bought. The World Wildlife Fund arranged the manufacture and delivery of boxes. The wildlife branch of the Forestry Commission selected six localities for a substantial experiment. Many officers of the Forestry Commission have enthusiastically provided considerable resources to facilitate the smooth running of the project.

The experiment was designed to test whether bats preferred boxes facing north, east, south or west, positioned high or low on trees, and what degree of exposure was favoured. Eight boxes (four at three metres and four at five metres) were attached to 60 trees in each of six forests from northern Scotland to southern England. The results of the initial experiment, which ran for eight years, form the basis of the advice contained in this booklet.

The project continues with boxes being sited in the pattern described earlier, that is three boxes per tree. Now the aim is to find how bat populations adapt to the cropping and management of the forests.

On one occasion bats were observed entering boxes on the first evening after installation, and bats were first caught whilst roosting in them about five months later. By October 1990, over 3,000 bats had been ringed, representing seven of Britain's 15 resident species. Five species bred in the boxes: brown long-eared bat, *Plecotus auritus*, Pipistrelle *Pipistrellus pipistrellus*, noctule *Nyctalus noctula*, Leisler's *Nyctalus leisleri* and Natterer's *Myotis nattereri*. Several notable records were made including considerable distributional range extensions in northern England and Scotland. In Wareham Forest one brown long-eared bat was recovered from the same box at the same site 14 times between 1970 and 1987 and another 43 times in the same area over ten years. The nationally rare Leisler's bat bred in boxes in Cannock, and occurred in Thetford Forest eight years after the boxes were first sited. Also, in 1984, one adult female Leisler's marked in Cannock in 1980 was found dead in Exeter 250km (157 miles) to the SSW.

In other privately run projects elsewhere in Britain, Daubenton's bats *Myotis daubentonii* have had nurseries in boxes but no breeding clusters of other species have been reported to date.

Summary of bats ringed between 1976 and 1990 in six forests

Over 8,000 bats of seven species have been handled in this continuing experiment.

Forest / Bat species	Ardross	Bramshill	Cannock	Kielder	Thetford	Wareham	Total
Brown long-eared *Plecotus auritus*	37	100	156	5	712	883	1,893
Pipistrelle *Pipistrellus pipistrellus*	2	37	60	9	314	264	686
Noctule *Nyctalus noctula*	-	4	56	-	102	30	192
Leisler's *Nyctalus leisleri*	-	-	22	-	12	-	34
Whiskered *Myotis mystacinus*	-	-	2	2	-	8	12
Brandt's *Myotis brandtii*	-	-	3	2	-	1	6
Natterer's *Myotis nattereri*	2	-	-	1	3	225	231
Totals	41	141	299	19	1,143	1,411	3,054

Ardross   - 20 miles north of Inverness. Experiment terminated 1982.
Keilder   - 13 miles south east of Hawick - Scottish/English border. Experiment terminated 1982.
Cannock   - 20 miles north of Birmingham - Midlands. Modified experiment continues.
Bramshill - 6 miles north west of Aldershot - North Hampshire. Experiment terminated 1986.
Wareham   - 6 miles west of Poole, Dorset - South coast. Modified and greatly extended.
Thetford - 3 miles west of Thetford - Norfolk. Experiment greatly extended and continues.

BIBLIOGRAPHY

DIETERICH, J. 1982. Vergleichende Beobachtungen über den Fledermausbesatz in verschiendenen Nistgeraten nach Untersuchungen in Schleswig-Holstein. *Myotis* 20, 38-44.

FEU, C. du. 1986. *Nest Boxes*. BTO Field Guide No 20. The Nunnery, Nunnery Place, Thetford, Norfolk, IP24 2PU. 72pp.

GERELL, R. 1981. Bat conservation in Sweden. *Myotis*, 18/19, 11-15.

ISSEL, B. & ISSEL, W. 1955. Versuche zur Ansiedlung von Waldfledermäusen in Fledermauska. sten. *Forstwiss zentralbl*, 74, 193-204.

JOLYET, A. 1918. Càbanes à chauves-souris. *Revue Eaux et Forêts*, 56, 121-126.

NAGEL, A. 1982. Ein neuer kasten für Fledermäusen. *Myotis*, 20, 45-47.

ROER, H. ed. 1968. *Myotis*, 6.

SCHOBER, W., & GRIMMBERGER, E. 1989. *A Guide to Bats in Britain and Europe*. Hamlyn, London.

STEBBINGS, R. E. 1974. Artificial roosts for bats. *Q. J. Devon Trust for Nature Conservation*, 6, 114-119.

STEBBINGS, R. E. 1986a. *Which Bat is it?* The Mammal Society, London.

STEBBINGS, R. E. 1986b. *Bats*. Anthony Nelson, Oswestry.

STEBBINGS, R. E. 1988. *Conservation of European Bats*. Christopher Helm, London.

USEFUL ADDRESSES

The Bat Conservation Trust, c/o The Conservation Foundation, 1 Kensington Gore, London SW7 2AR

English Nature, Northminster House, Peterborough PE1 1UA

Fauna and Flora Preservation Society, c/o Zoological Society of London, Regents Park, London NW1 4RY

The Mammal Society, Dept Zool, University of Bristol, Woodland Road, Bristol BS8 1UG

The **Robert Stebbings Consultancy Limited**, 74 Alexandra Road, Peterborough PE1 3DG

The Royal Society for Nature Conservation, The Green, Witham Park, Waterside South, Lincoln LN5 7JR

The Vincent Wildlife Trust, 10 Lovat Lane, London EC3R 8DT